Angels
All
Around Us

Helping Others
Through Hard Times

Ellen Pill Blooming, Ph.D.
Christine Dallman
June Eaton
Marie D. Jones
Carol McAdoo Rehme
Carol Stigger

Publications International, Ltd.

Contributing Writers:

Ellen Pill Blooming, Ph.D., is contributing editor for *Discovery Girls* magazine. She has collaborated on numerous inspirational books, including *Blessed by an Angel, Echoes of Love: Baby, God's Promise for Teens, Church Chuckles,* and *Toasts for Any Occasion.* Her stories and articles have been published in *Whispers from Heaven* and *Girl's Life* magazines. Dr. Blooming currently has two feature-length screenplays in the works.

Christine Dallman is the author of *Daily Devotions for Seniors* and a contributor to numerous other publications, including *How to Let God Help You Through Hard Times* and *One-Minute Bible Devotions.* She currently resides in Everett, WA.

June Eaton, an extensively published author, has contributed to over 20 books, and her articles and stories have appeared in more than 50 Christian periodicals. She is also a teacher with an M.A. from Northwestern University.

Marie D. Jones is an ordained minister and a contributing author to numerous books, including the *Echoes of Love* series, *Mother's Daily Prayer Book,* and *When You Lose Someone You Love: A Year of Comfort.* She is also the creator/ producer of Gigglebug Farms Simply Storybook Children's Videos.

Carol McAdoo Rehme, a firm believer in the power of stories, publishes prolifically in the inspirational market. Her inspirational and humorous stories appear widely in anthologies, series books, magazines, and national publications. A freelance author, editor, and ghostwriter, she has coauthored seven books. The latest is *Chicken Soup for the Empty Nester's Soul* (2008).

Carol Stigger is an award-winning communications consultant, teacher, and freelance writer specializing in international social justice issues and travel. Her inspirational work appears in several publications, including *Christian Science Monitor, Guideposts, Chicago Tribune, Vital Christianity,* and *Providence Journal.* She is also author of *Opportunity Knocks.*

Acknowledgments:

All Scripture quotations are taken from *The Holy Bible, New International Version.* Copyright © 1973, 1978, 1984, International Bible Society. Used by permission of Zondervan Publishing House. All rights reserved.

Cover photos: **PhotoDisc** (inset); **DigitalVision**

Contents

Helping Others Through Hard Times

The angel of the Lord encamps around those who fear him, and he delivers them. Psalm 34:7, NIV

Loneliness, fear, loss, failure, ruin, heartbreak: Life's most bitter pills are never ones we would choose, and yet they are administered to us, engulfing us in pain. Sometimes we can see the pain coming; other times it blindsides us. Either way, it threatens to turn us numb or raw or bitter, often causing us to recoil even from the touch that would heal us. That's when they show up: the angels God sends to encircle us, to set up a protective camp around us, and to gently walk us into our healing.

Angels All Around Us: Helping Others Through Hard Times is a book of stories, quotes, and prayers that will crack open the door, allowing a peek into the special ministry of angels whom God assigns to help his children through life's troubles. The stories are accounts from people just like you who have struggled, wept, ached, feared. As you read, perhaps your own heart will be opened to the possibility, if not the reality, of angels who are sent to gently tend wounded souls.

As you glance through this book, you will find stories of varying lengths. Some are just one or two pages long and can be read as a quick inspiration to begin your day or to give you a lift during a coffee or lunch break. Longer stories are three and four pages and make for good quiet time or bedtime reading. Quotes and prayers are interspersed throughout each section to give you food for thought and opportunities to reflect more deeply on the significance and meaning of the ministry of angels who attend us as we are walking through life's painful places.

Depending on your personal difficulties or the trials you've faced along your way, you may feel yourself drawn to a particular story in the book. Go ahead and start there. Part of the beauty of this volume is that it's not necessary to read it straight through. Each story can stand alone. Begin where you believe your heart will find the comfort and encouragement it needs. Each contributor to this book shares the same hope: that your faith will be renewed by the angels encamped around your life this moment, working faithfully to bring about your healing.

WHEN LIFE SEEMS DARKEST AND WE FEEL LOST AND ALL ALONE, THAT IS WHEN WE ARE MOST SURROUNDED BY ANGELS WHO CARE FOR US. ALL WE NEED TO DO IS OPEN OUR HEARTS TO SEE THEM REACHING OUT TO US WITH LOVE.

Secret Scripture Angel

Blanche was in her twenties when a powerful depression gripped her. Employed across the country, far from friends and family members, a situation at work was making her feel utterly trapped. When her alarm went off in the morning, Blanche wanted to stay in bed, or escape down the shower drain, or just go past the office and keep on driving. Instead, with great loathing, she took her place at her desk, sinking that much deeper into the quicksand of her despair.

It had been her lifetime habit to read her Bible. Now, however, when she most needed it, she found herself unable or unwilling to pick it up. Somehow the hope that it would be of help had ebbed from her heart.

One morning as she sat down at her desk, a little slip of paper caught her eye. Picking it up, she read the passage of Scripture on it. It was just a few verses, but it shed a beam of much-needed encouragement into her thoughts. Every day for the next several weeks, a new passage showed up on her desk. The scraps of paper were her lifeline to the truth of God's goodness and love, a lifeline pulling her back toward the shore of hope.

It took months before the situation at work was resolved, but Blanche's depression had already begun to melt. Slowly, like an iceberg, her heaviness dissolved into the sea of her days. Although her Scripture angel could not possibly have known what that little foray of encouragement did to create a turning point for her soul, Blanche will never forget it.

An Angel's Arms

If it hadn't been for my son, I would've been ready to say, "Okay, I've had enough of this life." I was drowning in the depths of despair. My son was in college, so it would have been easy to convince myself that he no longer needed me. But I knew he did, especially after losing his father to ALS.

My husband had died just four weeks before. We struggled together for three years while Lou Gehrig's disease took away his abilities to walk, to move, to eat; ultimately it robbed him of the ability to breathe. And through it all, his mind remained clear, allowing him to know exactly what was happening. ALS is a nightmare.

Of course, everyone thought that the nightmare had finally ended when he died. Why didn't they understand that it was just a new battle beginning for me? I had lost everything. All I had done for three years was take care of my sweetheart. He was my very best friend. My love. My life. And since, for the past year, I'd only been able to leave the house when a hospice worker was staying with him, he'd really become my only friend. He was all I had.

After he died, there had been a lot to do at first, but then things settled down. All the friends and family went home. My son went back to college. People assumed I was okay. They thought I must be relieved to no longer have the burden of caring for my husband, but all I wanted was to have him back. I wanted my best friend. I wanted the love of my life. I wanted things to be the way they were.

I sank into a dark depression and felt totally hollow and empty. I wasn't eating or sleeping. For the past year I had slept on the couch, next to my husband's hospital bed. Now it was the only place I was able to get any rest at all. It seemed impossible to sleep in the darkness of night, but sometimes I could get a few hours of rest in the early morning, after dawn. I would curl up on my couch and let exhaustion take over.

One early morning, I had just closed my eyes when I felt it. It was like a warm blanket . . . first on my legs, then covering my entire body. As I turned on my side, it seemed to enfold me. Then I realized what I felt. It was a hug. Arms were reaching around me, holding me. I didn't feel scared. I felt such comfort and peace that I don't know how to find the words to explain it. I *knew* that I was being held by an angel. For the first time in weeks, I smiled. I felt full inside, and I felt loved. I knew I was going to make it through . . . everything was going to be okay.

I fell sound asleep with those heavenly arms around me. I slept better than I had in weeks and woke feeling rested and hopeful. It hasn't been an easy journey, and I know that I've still got a long way to go down this difficult path. But whenever things get overwhelming and I feel that it's just too much to bear, I remember the night when an angel hugged me tight. Then my strength, courage, and hope return.

EACH OF US HAS AN ANGEL NEARBY. ALWAYS.

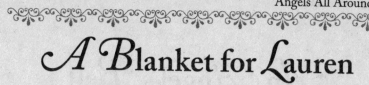

A Blanket for Lauren

This is how anguish feels, Kim decided. *Numb. Hollow. Cold.*

She stared at the still infant on her bed. These next few minutes would encompass the entire extent of their time together. This was the first—and last—motherly thing she would ever do for baby Lauren.

"I have to do...something," she'd tried to express her desperate desire earlier. The nurse had nodded, abruptly left the room, and returned with a delicate box.

"Women from a local congregation make and donate these," she explained. "Take all the time you need." The door whispered shut behind her.

Kim opened the hand-painted lid and brushed aside a layer of pink tissue paper. She gasped as she lifted out a receiving blanket, milky white and cloud soft. Next, she unfolded a tiny rosebud sleeper. Suppressing a sob, she held it to her chest before setting it aside to reach for the daintily crocheted hat.

Humming a lullaby, Kim reached for the lifeless body of her premature daughter. She shut her mind to the dreams she'd had for the future. Instead, she willed herself to be present in the *now,* this moment with her precious little one.

With trembling fingers, she tenderly dressed Lauren. Only when she cuddled the chenille-wrapped infant close to her heart, did she discover the message of comfort—hand-embroidered by some understanding mother—along the blanket's edge:

A fleeting moment in your arms, but in your heart forever.
And Kim let her tears flow.

An Angel's Bell

Some people believe that when a bell rings, an angel gets its wings. In this case, the sound of a doorbell meant an angel was near.

The Chapman family was having a rough time. Max had lost his job as a foreman when the factory closed down. Doris didn't make enough at her drugstore job to feed and clothe their family of six—nine if you counted the dog, cat, and bunny! The family had sold their big house and traded down. They survived on food stamps.

Max was trying to find work, but the holidays were approaching and it looked like nothing would open up until January. It became a question of just making it through the holidays. They all had a solid faith, and Max and Doris were really proud of how the kids handled the hard times. Everyone understood that there would be no gifts or holiday meals. They agreed that this year they'd celebrate the true meaning of Christmas.

And then the doorbell rang. No one was there—just huge boxes of presents and food. Someone had delivered Christmas! It proved to be the best Christmas the Chapmans ever had.

Max got a new job in January, and before long they were back to their previous standard of living. Every year from then on, the family would anonymously deliver Christmas to someone who was having a difficult time. They never did learn who had supplied their feast and gifts that year. They just liked to think it was their angel.

IN THE COMPANY OF ANGELS, EVERY PROBLEM HAS A SOLUTION, EVERY CHALLENGE A LESSON, EVERY CLOUD A SILVER LINING. IN THE COMPANY OF ANGELS, TROUBLES ARE DIMINISHED, TRIALS ARE OVERCOME, AND LIFE BECOMES A BLESSING AGAIN.

Father,

It's easy to say, "Let me know if there's anything I can do." But how much better to peer closer, assess the situation to find what needs doing…then simply do *it. Help me look into a friend's needs instead of waiting to be asked. Help me replace the words I utter so glibly with actions that might matter even more.*

Amen

IN THE MIRACLE OF EACH NEW DAY, AN ANGEL IS BORN.

A Way to Walter's Heart

A little boy named Benjamin came fluttering on angel's wings into Walter's life one day. Walter had been fighting cancer for about six years at that point, and he was tired from the battle. He had never been much of a churchgoer, but he had been attending with his wife for the past several months when he felt well enough to do so. In the past he had consistently turned down his family's invitations to church and had brushed aside their conversations about God. But recently he felt the need to take these things more seriously. Though he tried to avoid his fear of death by simply not thinking about it, he was starting to think about it more and more despite his best efforts not to.

Conventional religion had left a bad taste in Walter's mouth as a youngster. He wanted nothing of that sort of thing. It seemed irrational, then, to walk through the doors of a church, but maybe there was something there he'd missed all those years ago. Regardless of all that, what could it hurt to sit in the pew and sing a few songs and listen to the preacher for half an hour? It was a chance to be with his family, if nothing else.

But much to his surprise, Walter ended up meeting an angel in church, a little blond boy who shook Walter's hand one morning and beamed when Walter slipped him a caramel. Benjamin became Walter's every-Sunday angel. Candy or no candy from Walter, Benjamin had a huge hug for the elderly man and at some point began calling him "grandpa."

Benjamin would phone Walter during the week to see how he was feeling. When Walter landed in the hospital with one of his frequent bouts with pneumonia, Benjamin would ask his mom to take him to visit his grandpa. It was clear to Walter's family that Benjamin had stolen Walter's heart, and it had done him a world of good to have those Sunday morning hugs to look forward to.

Then one day, after Walter had returned home from a brief stay in the hospital, Benjamin urged his mom to take him to visit Walter at home. Because the boy was so insistent, his mom called and arranged the visit.

Leaning over the arm of Walter's armchair, Benjamin looked at the old man's face intently and quietly asked him, "Grandpa, do you know that you are going to see God soon?"

Walter's heart was tender now, and he shook his head.

"Can you tell him that I love him when you see him?" the little boy asked.

"Yes, I'll tell him all about what a wonderful kid you are," Walter replied.

"I tell him all about you when I say my prayers at night," Benjamin said.

Tears streamed down Walter's face as he opened his heart to God that day. The change in him was unmistakable. How freely he was able to show his affection for his family now. How joyfully he sang the songs of praise in church. How peacefully he passed into eternity soon afterward. How good of God to send the faith of that tender young angel to lead him home.

Hands Off

Acceptance, he'd been told. That was the key—to accept his lot in life.

Well, he had, hadn't he? At least up to a point. He accepted responsibility for the daredevil foolishness that caused the accident. He accepted the reality of the accident that caused his paralysis. He accepted the paralysis that meant nothing on his body from his shoulders down worked anymore. He even accepted that his life depended fully on the ventilator that breathed for him and on his parents who saw to his needs.

From surgery to rehab to more surgeries and finally to home, the road he'd traveled had challenged him. He had owned up to it, even at his lowest lows. What Rick couldn't accept was the loss of his art. That hurt too much. Art defined him; he was good at it. *Was. Was good at it.*

For as long as he could remember, Rick had loved to draw. He'd gotten his first art award in kindergarten. From then on, he knew what he wanted to do and he did it. His friends teased that his pencil was like a permanent appendage. He doodled on the corners of his school papers. He sketched animals and landscapes, uproarious caricatures of his friends, and serious portraits of his family members. He volunteered to paint pep rally posters for the high school teams. At college he had designed sets for musicals. *He'd done it . . . in the past tense.*

But the past wasn't the here and now. Except, apparently, to his mother. She'd been there—from quarterback to quadriplegic—cheering and championing her only son, always with the highest expectations. When he mastered the suck-and-puff

control on his computerized wheelchair, she beamed with the same pride she'd shown for his winning college football team. When she heard about "mouth artists," she researched the details, determined that her son could compete with any of them.

Rick considered the easel mounted near the sunny window. He blew into the straw to propel his wheelchair a tad closer.

She had stabilized the paper and explained the process earlier. "Look here, Ricky, these levers move the easel up and down, right and left," she said. "You can even make it tilt."

She pointed at the bracket where the mouth stick rested. "See how it clamps the pencil? Just grab it with your lips."

"What, and draw? You think it's that easy, Mom?"

"Well, maybe not easy, but you can do anything you set your mind to."

"Maybe. Once upon a time. But not now."

"Rick, when you were in college, you told me your art 'comes from the inside.' If you really believe that, hands shouldn't be necessary." She ruffled his hair and walked toward the kitchen. "Just give it a try, won't you?"

Rick closed his eyes. *I don't need any more reminders of what I've lost. It hurts too much.*

Recent images flashed in his mind, scenes from all the inspirational film clips his mom had played for him: Servicemen who lost limbs and returned to military duty with prosthetics; Denver comedian Josh Blue who forged a successful career despite his condition; amputees and people with spinal injuries involved in paralympic sports. She reminded him about the doctors—the neurologists, the specialists—who pointed them to medical findings that claimed brain signals could reroute and find new paths to do old things.

Obviously, his mom had been priming him for this moment, daring him to attempt the impossible. Wanting him to believe that he could train his mouth to attempt what his hands once did so effortlessly. What did she think she was, his own personal angel?

Well, he'd show her what was possible . . . and impossible . . . without hands.

Rick puckered his lips around the mouth stick and stabilized it with his teeth. He pulled his chin in, toward his neck, and watched the line scratch down the paper.

Stupid, he criticized.

He raised his chin and drew a line upward. *Shaky.*

So he tried a side-to-side move. He experimented with arcs. He toyed with circles. He remembered the pointillism technique he'd learned in college art classes and began stippling the paper with dots. He worked to finesse his mouth and head movements until he managed to complete a dense area of dots.

With a little more practice, he thought in awe, *this might really work.*

The possibility astounded him. Creative excitement bubbled within, charging him with an energy he hadn't felt in years. Maybe, just maybe, he could find and retool that artistic part of himself he thought he'd lost.

Rick worked a few more minutes at the easel until he'd drawn and shaded a crude heart. Then, replacing the stick in its bracket, he hollered over his shoulder, "Mom? Mom?" He grinned when she came running and nodded at the drawing.

"Look, Ma," he beamed, "no hands!"

Angel Grandma

Grandma Meda was 98 years old when her son, Lara's father, died suddenly of mesothelioma, a lung cancer associated with exposure to asbestos. Lara was devastated. Just months ago Lara had buried her own son, who had been only 23 years old.

Grandma Meda, still an avid crocheter, had already created afghans for many of her family members, as well as for most of the shut-ins from her church. Now she wanted to do something special for her grieving granddaughter, Lara.

As soon as her son, Lara's father, died, Grandma began to create a beautiful, pure white Victorian-style afghan. With each stitch she said a prayer for her son and all his family. She crocheted throughout that day and the next. She seemed to gain consolation from the repetition of the stitches and the transformation of the yarn into a work of art.

Time was getting short and she still had a long way to go. But then the funeral was delayed and she had just enough time to finish.

Lara drove more than 300 miles to attend the ceremony, and she had been up all night working on the eulogy. She was exhausted. When she arrived, she headed for her grandma, enveloping her in hugs. Then the two sat holding hands.

When Grandma Meda gave her the exquisite afghan, Lara was overwhelmed with emotion. "Oh, Gram," was all she could say. She ran her hand over the fine, even stitches and gazed in wonder at the work of one so advanced in years.

After the funeral, where she delivered the eulogy, Lara sat down with Grandma, pulled the warm, cozy blanket over both of them, and the two continued to console each other on the loss of son and father.

"When my brother and I were kids," Lara remembered, "Gram, you laughed with us when we were happy and consoled us when we were sad. Imagine, at 98, you still know how to make us all feel better. You are still living, but you already have your halo," Lara said to her grandmother, whose soft, white, curly hair formed a perfect circle around her head.

**ANGEL WINGS SHELTER AND PROTECT US
UNTIL WE ARE READY TO LEARN HOW TO FLY.**

God,

Bless the unknown angels who clear the cluttered paths of the lost, who wipe the tears of the grieving, and who hold the hands that tremble in fear. Their names may be known only to you, but their acts of mercy give me the assurance that your love touches everyone, everywhere.

Amen

Angel Babies

"We can try again later, honey," Tom whispered. But Sandy wasn't sure she would ever recover from this miscarriage. It was her third in four years, and she was beginning to believe that she and her husband would never have the gift of a precious child.

Sandy went to bed that night crying. Tom held her close, but he soon drifted off to sleep. Sandy was alone again to face her grief and sense of failure. Why couldn't her body nurture a baby through to birth? She wept silently, feeling as though the entire world was crashing down around her.

A soft breeze blew across her face, and Sandy sat up, thinking she had left a window open. Her eyes caught a gentle glowing light at the foot of the bed. She sat very still as the light came closer, and Sandy gasped as the shape of a person took form. No, not a person, she realized, but a beautiful angel surrounded by an aura of white light.

The angel was holding out her arms, and in her arms were two gorgeous babies, both sleeping soundly. Their eyelids fluttered and Sandy felt her hand go to her heart as she began to weep. She looked up at the angel, who was smiling back at her and nodding gently.

When Sandy woke the next morning, she called for Tom and grabbed his hand, squeezing it. She recounted the events of the night before—not sure now if it had been a dream. But either way, she once again had hope.

"Yes, we will try again," she said, smiling.

Ten months later, Sandy gave birth to healthy twins.

Angels for the Children

Denise remembered the childhood fear that would paralyze her when her father's anger would rise up. She could not think how to answer his booming demands for an explanation when she was in trouble. There was rarely any disobedience on the part of her or her older sister; they were too afraid to misbehave. Even the perception of bad behavior was not tolerated.

One time, as a five-year-old, Denise had crept out of bed to see who had come knocking at their door so late at night. She and her sister, Clara, could hear a woman sobbing, and Clara had convinced Denise to go see who it was. Although the girls were under orders never to leave their beds once tucked in, Denise ventured a peek into the living room and immediately met her father's stern gaze as her mother was offering a tissue to the distraught woman. Hours later, Denise was pulled from bed and spanked until her backside nearly bled. This was how discipline was meted out during Denise's childhood.

As an adult, Denise still found herself stuttering and near tears any time she was questioned or challenged by an authority figure, especially if it was a man. Despite her best efforts to be rational, she could not keep her composure. She hated this weakness not only because it was embarrassing for her, but also because it was awkward for those who were merely trying to talk with her about issues at hand.

After one particularly humiliating encounter, Denise prayed to somehow be set free from the irrational fear that would sweep over her. In the days that followed that prayer, she found herself humming the refrain of an old song that had filled her mind. When she stopped to recall the lyrics, they came to her, along with the memory of an old picture that used to hang on the wall at her grandmother's home. The picture was of a frightened little girl and boy crossing a rickety bridge together, a storm gathering around them. Unseen by them, yet close behind, was a guardian angel, large and strong, dominating the picture and gently guiding them along their way. The song lyrics to the lullaby Denise had been humming came up from somewhere far back in her memory: "All night, all day/Angels watchin' over me, my Lord/All night, all day,/ Angels watchin' over me."

It occured to Denise that even in the anxious days of her childhood there had been protection and comfort for her along her way. Upon reflection, it was perhaps a miracle that she had come into adulthood relatively whole considering the abuses that had been intended to shape her character. After a time of pondering these things, a curious change began to take place in her ability to interact with authority figures. In situations that used to evoke those childish fears, it was as if she could sense the protective presence of the angel that had guarded her in childhood, making it safe for her to be the grown-up she needed to be in situations that had intimidated her. It happened subtly but surely, and today there is almost no trace of the shuddering child from her past.

Then one day, the words of Jesus in the Book of Matthew caught Denise's attention and confirmed to her what she'd come to understand: "See that you do not look down on one of these little ones. For I tell you that their angels in heaven always see the face of my Father in heaven" (18:10, NIV). There are, indeed, angels for the children.

Birthday Blues

"**D**arrin is worse than ever, Vicky," said Ken. "We've got to do something."

"Something?" Vicky's bitter laugh rose with a note of hysteria. "Something?"

Her husband shrugged. "Maybe we've overlooked . . ."

"Something."

"Yes. His recent decline is obvious. The doctors can't pinpoint the reason, so it's up to us. I say we try to figure it out and fix it."

Vicky knew exactly what Ken meant. Darrin's weight kept falling, and he was in a blue funk, the worst they'd seen in years.

Long before he was diagnosed with Friedreich's ataxia so many years ago, it seemed as though their son was always falling down. He was clumsier than his grade-school friends.

"You just need to grow into your feet," they teased.

Darrin's problem escalated to difficulty running, descending stairs, keeping his balance. He had trouble with buttons and holding a pencil. They consulted specialists and received the final verdict when Darrin turned 12: He had a neuromuscular disease. Insidious. Progressive. Incurable.

Disbelief came first—with horror, numbness, guilt, and blame following hot on its heels. Yet they weathered it all. Cane and crutches. Spinal fusion to stabilize his scoliosis. Struggles to make his slurring speech understood. Walker and wheelchair. And, now, an electric cart.

With his 30th birthday approaching, Darrin moved from an assisted-living facility to a specially equipped apartment. Ken and Vicky interviewed and hired health aides to assist their son with his personal needs. Yet a dark shadow hovered.

Instead of celebrating this long-desired level of independence, Darrin was depressed. He was irritable and angry at best, sullen and unresponsive the rest of the time. He refused to go outside. His appetite waned. He needed *something* to perk him up.

"Ken, I think I've figured it out!" Vicky's enthusiasm was exultant. "Darrin needs to be responsible for someone besides himself."

"What?"

"Don't you see? This disease encourages introspection. He needs to focus outward instead of inward all the time. He needs someone to care for."

"What about a dog?"

Vicky nodded. "But it could be years before Darrin gets to the top of the waiting list for a service animal. Why wait? Companionship could be more valuable at this point than physical assistance."

Ken squeezed his wife's hand. "It'll be our birthday gift!"

A puppy would be impractical, they agreed, so they scouted for an adult animal. They contacted family, friends, and volunteers. They even placed an ad in a Friedreich's ataxia newsletter and were amazed at the response. It appeared there were lots of dogs up for adoption, waiting to be loved. But they chose Ollie.

A sweetheart of a dog, Ollie was a mild-mannered golden retriever who had flunked her training at Colorado Canine Companions.

"Flunked?" Vicky giggled at the thought. But it was true. Ollie had sailed through months of extensive training necessary to become a valuable assistance dog only to—as the trainer joked—"fail her finals." In the end, she was found to be too playful. Too often, rather than retrieve an object, she rebelled with a joyous stubbornness and tossed it around in a one-dog game of catch.

"Well, their loss is Darrin's gain," Ken commented when they brought Ollie home. He and Vicky fell in love with the dog's sweet personality overnight and counted the days until their son's birthday. It was hard to keep such an exciting secret.

In the meantime, they outfitted Ollie with all the necessities—kennel, bed, rawhide chews, food and water bowls, toys...lots of toys for her to retrieve and toss to her heart's content. On the appointed day, they loaded the van and drove to Darrin's apartment.

Ken held a finger to his lips, silently turned the knob, and motioned Ollie ahead of them through the door.

Darrin sat in his electric cart, engrossed at the computer in the far corner of the room and unaware of their presence. They watched Ollie pad across the thick carpet toward their son and sit obediently beside his chair.

Darrin started. "Whaaaaat?"

"Happy Birthday!" chorused his parents.

Ollie responded with a thump of her tail.

Darrin frowned. "Whose...dog?"

"Yours," said Ken. "Ollie, meet Darrin. Darrin, meet Ollie."

"A dog? You...got me...a dog?" He recoiled when Ollie placed a friendly paw on his thin thigh.

"Sure. You're going to love her. She's a real sweetheart!"

"No, thanks."

Ken raised his brows at his son's curtness. "Wait 'til you see her retrieve. She's a real go-getter!" he enthused.

"Not...interested."

Disgusted at the rude attitude, his dad opened his mouth. But he clamped it shut when Ollie nudged her head under Darrin's long hand. She leaned her weight on his lap and nuzzled her damp nose against his still fingers.

Vicky held her breath. Ken bit his lip. They exchanged pensive glances over their son's head.

And then it happened. A hesitant move of his fingers. A lift of his wrist. A slow stroke along the length of Ollie's large head. The dog's eyes drifted shut when Darrin continued stroking.

"Good...girl." Darrin's face softened for the first time in weeks. The shadow was lifting.

He looked up at his parents and a smile slowly spread across his face "Did you...bring cake?"

**WHEN YOU TURN OFF A LIGHT,
REMEMBER TO TURN ON A PRAYER.**

Ruby

John grieved the loss of his beloved dog, Ruby. After his wife, Marian, had passed away, Ruby had been his constant companion, helping him heal, sitting at his feet when he read, and walking with him through the woods by the cabin they called home. Now Ruby was gone, and John felt so alone.

As night fell, John wondered how he would sleep without Ruby at the foot of his bed, nestled in blankets, snoring softly. The German shepherd had been a big dog, but so loving and gentle.

The next morning, John decided to take a long walk after newly fallen snow had blanketed the area. The air was cold and crisp, filling John's lungs as the snow gave way softly beneath his feet. He walked up a grade and drank in the view of the fields beyond, now draped in snow, and he ached for the company of his old pal, Ruby. He imagined her running down into the snow, rolling and barking happily.

John went back to his cabin, sat down on the bed, and wept. As he cried, he felt the sensation of something jump up onto the bed. John was startled to see a distinct depression in the outer quilt, as if something was sitting there. And then he heard it, the gentle snoring he knew so well.

He wanted to reach out and touch Ruby, but he knew she would not be there, not in a physical sense. John smiled through his tears as he realized Ruby would always be with him, like a canine angel, watching over him and reminding him that he was never truly alone.

Apple Pie Angel

Amanda found it difficult to know what to say to someone who was ill, especially when the person was her favorite uncle and the illness was terminal. So the week before Thanksgiving, she found herself asking him the first thing that popped into her mind.

"What would you like me to make for the family Thanksgiving dinner, to go with the turkey and mashed potatoes, Uncle Tim?"

He thought a bit, then answered: "You know, I haven't had a good homemade apple pie in a long time. How about baking one for me?"

"Done!" she agreed. She had no idea at the time exactly what she was getting herself into.

The trouble was, Amanda had never baked a pie before. She wondered what she had been thinking to agree to Uncle Tim's request. If she was going to make a decent pie in the next week, she'd have to get busy and practice.

With one finger holding the page down on her cookbook, she threw the ingredients together. Then she rolled out the dough on the kitchen counter. It looked fine, but when she went to pick up the crust, it stuck on the counter and broke up into dozens of little globs. She had to scrape up the whole mess and throw it in the garbage.

On her second try, she put plenty of flour on the counter, but the circle of dough was too small, so she gathered it up and started over.

This time she used waxed paper on both sides of the dough and marked the spot the dough had to reach in order to be big enough. Then she negotiated her rolling pin to spread the crust into a circle. Finally, she was successful, so she cut up the apples, sprinkled them with sugar and cinnamon, and baked her first pie.

The feeling of success was nothing compared to the experience of watching Uncle Tim dig into his second piece of pie on Thanksgiving Day. Amanda was so pleased, she promised him another pie on Christmas. Again, he ate two pieces.

For Valentine's Day, encouraged again by her uncle's reaction, Amanda baked him a pie with a heart-shape design cut out of the top crust. He grinned and thanked her, but he seemed tired and he ate only one piece this time. The rest he put away for the remainder of the week.

Tim often told his daughter how much it meant to him to have Amanda bake those pies for him. He said that when he looked at her, she seemed all shiny like an angel.

"Hmmm... maybe it's your medication affecting your eyesight," the daughter suggested.

"Don't think so," he murmured before he fell asleep.

In the period between Valentine's Day and Easter, Uncle Tim seemed to deteriorate rapidly. His appetite diminished and his doctor said the family should start thinking about hospice care.

Hesitantly, Amanda asked just before the holiday weekend: "Want another apple pie for Easter dinner, Uncle Tim?"

"You better believe it," he said, sounding more enthusiastic than he looked. "Goes good with ham."

Amanda managed a sad smile at dinner on Sunday as she watched this once-robust man slowly taking little bites of food. He barely finished a whole slice of the pie she had so lovingly made. He was tiring more quickly and eating less and less as his breathing became shallower.

On her next visit, Amanda was afraid he might not be around for Father's Day, but she asked him anyway:

"How about another pie for the big day, Uncle Tim?"

"I haven't been too hungry lately. . . . I'll let you know," he whispered as he leaned back on his pillow and closed his eyes.

"Okay, Unc." She tried to keep her voice even. "I'll have the bag of apples ready. Just give me the word."

A few weeks later, Uncle Tim requested his pie, which Amanda made with as much love as she had, praying as she worked. "Lord, please watch over this dear man. Give him comfort and peace."

In July, the hospice team began to assemble and plans were made to move Tim from his daughter's home to his own for the final weeks of his life.

On July 4th, Amanda made her last pie for Tim. The family gathered for a cookout and Tim ate only a tiny wedge of pie, nothing else. He seemed distant and distracted but determined to go home to die.

When it was time to leave, Amanda talked to her uncle for the last time.

"I won't say good-bye, just see you later. I love you." He smiled weakly and she hugged his frail body.

"I love you, too," he answered. "And I'll be waiting to greet you in heaven."

The family told Amanda that in the end, her pie was the only food Tim could eat, and he downed it one sliver at a time. He died two weeks later.

Many times Amanda thought about the day she first asked her uncle what he'd like to eat, and her quick response to say yes, even though she'd never baked a pie. She thought she had just been foolish.

"Now," she says, "I know it was God nudging me to give comfort to a dying man. It was such a privilege."

WHEN GOD SENDS HIS ANGELS TO COMFORT US, WE CAN KNOW THEM BY THE HALLMARKS OF HIS LOVE IN THEIR ACTIONS, IN THEIR WORDS, AND ESPECIALLY IN THEIR TOUCH.

Our hearts are bruised, Father, black and blue from life's pounding. Swollen and sore from hurts real and imagined. We need a sooth-ing balm to ease our discomfort. Please send into our lives those who have healing hands and helping hearts, those who would salve our pain by word and deed.

Amen

What Is Lost Is Found

Only a parent could ever truly understand the fear and pain of knowing that their child is lost and alone. For Dean and Matty, that fear and pain threatened to overwhelm them the day their teenage daughter ran away from home. Diana was 17, headstrong, and had threatened to run away before when she couldn't get her way; this was the first time she made good on it, though. Now Dean and Matty had no way to get in touch with her. She was not answering her cell phone, and none of her friends had any idea where she was, if they were indeed telling the truth.

Dean blamed himself, for he and Diana had gotten into a big fight the day before, over some stupid thing Dean couldn't even recall. He and Diana seemed to butt heads so much lately, which was typical of parent-teen relationships. Matty told him not to blame himself and that everything would be okay, but the apprehension in her voice was obvious. They held each other close and cried.

When the police reported that Diana's car had been found on the side of a road ten miles to the north, fear turned into gut-wrenching panic. Dean and Matty took time off from work, unable to move from the couch by the phone in their living room. Friends and family came by to offer support, but as the days went on—and there was no word from Diana or the police—they began to feel hope slipping away.

One night, Matty lay in Dean's arms on the sofa. As Dean slept, Matty thought about how she would simply not be able to live anymore if Diana turned up dead. The very thought chilled her in a way nothing ever had. Her beloved only child, possibly dead . . . or worse. Matty shook and tried to fight back the onslaught of fresh tears, willing the phone to ring or the doorknob to turn, willing Diana to come bouncing into the room as if nothing had ever happened. Matty knew she could not take much more of this.

"God, please help me, please. Help my girl come home. Make sure she is safe," Matty whispered in prayer. As she did, a warmth came over her and she looked up to see a brilliant glowing figure standing before her, with arms outstretched.

"What is lost is found," the figure said in a voice that sounded more like a choir, a beautiful and lilting voice that made Matty's heart swell with gratitude.

The figure began to fade from view, but Matty swore she saw a pair of wings spreading out from the figure's back, and a soft halo of light above its head.

An angel! Matty thought. *Thank you, God, for sending me an angel.* For the first time in days, she slept through the night.

That morning, around 10 A.M., the phone rang. It was the local police. They had found Diana safe and sound at a local youth hostel. Diana got on the phone, crying and begging her parents to let her come home.

An hour later, Dean and Matty opened the door and cried out in joy. Diana rushed into their arms and apologized profusely, telling her parents she would never do such a thing again. But her parents didn't care—they were just glad to have her home. Matty hugged her daughter tightly, as she gratefully smiled at her husband.

Close Call

I was having trouble finding my angels. Life was spinning out of control. Even the people I shared my life with, my most precious blessings—my kids and my husband—were simply driving me crazy. All the good in life seemed to be obscured by a heavy fog.

I'd get together with friends, and we'd complain. It seemed our only bond was our mutual dissatisfaction with everything. At work, nothing was right. I'd sit with coworkers and complain. I'd talk to my boss and complain. I'm not sure how I got any work done amid all the complaining!

And I was always late. The elementary school principal wanted to know why my children were always late. I wanted to send a note saying: "Please excuse Emily and William because their mother simply cannot keep up with life." I never seemed to sit down or breathe. I'd begun to feel like I was going to snap in two.

Then one night I was coming home late from work. The highway between the town where I work and the town where I live is a hilly two-lane road with no shoulder. There's a deep ditch on either side. I was so tired I hadn't even bothered to turn the radio on to my usual oldies station. If I had, I might not have heard the voice.

I was heading up a hill and hit a patch of black ice. Everything happened in slow motion as I skidded into the oncoming lane. Just before I crested the hill, I prayed for the first time in ages. It was more like pathetic pleading, actually. There

was a lot of traffic that time of evening, and I wasn't able to get back into my own lane. I came over the top of the hill and a pickup truck was headed right for me. He was so close that I saw the look of panic on the driver's face. I'll never forget it. And then I heard it.

"I am with you." It was a female voice, clear as a bell, coming from nowhere. And once I heard it, I felt totally calm. I grasped the wheel firmly, tried once more and was able to get back into my own lane as I felt the whoosh of the truck streak past me. It's a miracle we didn't crash. And that was the key word. *Miracle.* I pulled off the first chance I had—a little diner at a crossroads. I practically ran out of my car and into the warmth of the little café. I sat down at the counter and ordered a cup of coffee. I didn't want to think about what had happened. My hands were shaking as I lifted the coffee to my lips.

"You okay?" the waitress asked.

"I was almost killed in an accident at the top of that last hill." I barely managed to get the words out.

"Head-on collision?" She guessed while wiping the counter next to me.

I nodded.

"Heard a voice, did you?" she casually inquired.

I dropped my coffee cup onto the counter. Hot coffee went everywhere.

"What did you say?" I was sure I had heard her wrong.

She wiped up the mess as she spoke. "You're the third or fourth person who has come in here saying they were saved from an accident in that same spot. The other drivers said they

heard a voice and then suddenly they were able to get out of the way just in time."

"That's ridiculous. I didn't hear anything." I put way too much money on the counter and ran out.

I fumbled to get my car keys in the door lock and happened to look up. The night sky was unbelievably beautiful. I hadn't really looked at the sky in *years*. I really looked at it now, and it was magnificent.

I got home safely and walked in the door. My kids were fighting and my husband was on the couch watching television. They barely looked up when I came in the door. I was overcome with my love for them. I was so thankful that I'd made it home. I hugged and kissed everyone—even the cat, who wasn't at all pleased with my show of affection.

"Listen up, everyone!" All activity stopped. They looked at me as if I was about to announce that there would be no supper for the rest of the week. "I want you all to know how much I love you." Silence. They didn't quite know what to think about my declaration. "AND . . . I think I'm in the mood to order some pizza!" *This* declaration was met with cheers.

I never could explain how I heard that voice and was able to get my car back into my own lane. I also can't explain how that moment changed me. Was it an angel who spoke to me in the car that night? I believe it was. Either way, something inside me forever changed. I breathe easier now. I seem to have more time. I remember how much I love my family. And I'm convinced that there's more to this life than meets the eye.

**WHEN IT'S TOO DARK TO SEE YOUR PATH—
TRUST YOUR ANGELS TO GUIDE YOU.**

Excuse me, God,

But it's pretty dark in here right now.
If it's not too much trouble,
I could sure use an angel or two
to help me see what's going on.
Just a little help to get me moving
in the right direction would be
so very much appreciated.
I know the dawn is coming,
I'm just not sure which direction
to turn to find it.

Love,
Me

Emergency Aloft

The trip sounded too good to be true for teachers Tim and Jen White: a week in Spain at a reasonable price during their school's spring break. Arranged by one of their colleagues, the trip included a group of 30 other teachers from their district.

They were to spend two days in Madrid, including a visit to *El Prado,* one of Europe's finest art museums; next the medieval city of Toledo, three days on the Costa del Sol, with a side trip to Granada's Moorish palace, the *Alhambra.* A quick trip across the Strait of Gibraltar to the Moroccan city of Tangier was their last stop.

It would be a wonderful educational experience they could later share with their students. The couple couldn't wait to begin. They boarded a plane at Chicago's O'Hare Airport and flew to New York, where they met their flight bound for Madrid.

"Instead of stewardesses, the Spanish jet swarmed with stewards," said Jen, "elegantly dressed, very formal gentlemen who were there to cater to our every whim. We felt like royalty."

Once they got into the air, the passengers began to relax and await their refreshments. The Whites chatted with their friends.

"About a half-hour into the flight," said Tim, "I noticed a flash of light and flames leaping up on the opposite side of the plane. Then there was a sudden explosion." Instantly the cabin became eerily quiet, and Tim remembered the stewards hurrying up and down the aisles, checking overhead bins, disappearing for awhile, then reappearing. "We tried to ask questions, but they wouldn't tell us a thing."

Jen and Tim clung tightly to one another with hearts pounding. Outwardly they tried to remain calm. "What can it be?" they wondered. "Are we in real danger?" Noise and excitement rose in the cabin, and then quickly turned to fear as the stewards busied themselves and studiously avoided eye contact or sharing information with the passengers.

"O Lord, please protect us and all of our fellow passengers tonight," Jen prayed. "Quiet our hearts and help us remain calm."

Suddenly the intercom crackled as the voice of the captain cut through the air.

"Ladies and gentlemen," he announced. "We have lost an engine. But don't worry, we have another one. We will return to the airport for repairs." That was all that was said. No instructions, no requests, and most notably, no further encouraging comments were forthcoming. The intercom clicked off.

Tim and Jen, along with the other passengers, gripped their armrests and tried not to panic. Murmurs rippled through the crowd. The plane made several wide circles, then did an about-face and headed home.

Unspoken questions lurked in the eyes of Jen, Tim, and their friends, but they all were silent. The plane droned on. "We held our breath and huddled together," Jen recalled, "afraid to say or do anything."

Tim looked at his watch and determined that they had flown for half an hour before the engine failure and that the

trip back was now approaching 45 minutes. He wondered aloud what happened to those extra 15 minutes.

"Remember when we were circling out over the ocean?" one of his friends whispered. "I think they were dumping fuel."

Jen shivered as she began to realize the seriousness of the situation. "Lord, we are putting ourselves in your hands," she prayed again. "Please send help."

A few moments later, passengers in the window seats cried out, "Look!" Those who could peered out the windows and saw what looked like a brightly lighted highway. It was the runway at JFK. Lined up for several miles, with red lights flashing, were dozens of emergency vehicles—ambulances, fire trucks, foam spreaders, and others, ready to escort the plane back to the gate.

"Chills ran through my body," Jen said. "It felt as though a whole company of angels stood ready to surround us with their protection."

Tim added, "We were thrilled to see those lights but frightened that something bad would happen before we could land."

As the wheels touched down, the passengers responded with cheers and whoops of joy. When they filed out of the plane, some burst into tears of relief.

But Jen just prayed, thanking God for sending that whole cadre of angels to end their nightmare.

The passengers were ushered into buses and taken to a remote part of the airport. After hours without food or drink and no information, the airline booked the planeload of tourists into the airport hotel for an overnight stay.

"We waited a day and a half," said Tim, "for another plane to come back from Spain to pick us up. Then finally we continued our trip."

The relief at still being alive only heightened their enjoyment of their shortened vacation, the group of teachers agreed. Some said they felt angels all around them, including the emergency workers and even the crew, who by trying to appear nonchalant, helped reduce the panic.

"We savored every moment of the trip," said Jen, "knowing that if God hadn't intervened, the story would have ended very differently for all of us."

WHEN A DAY I DREADED TURNED OUT TO BE A GOOD DAY AFTER ALL, I KNEW MY ANGEL WAS WORKING OVERTIME.

Angels on high,

Thank you for always being there for me in times of trouble, just as you are in times of joy. I know I can always turn to you for the wisdom and comfort I seek no matter what is going on in my life. I am so grateful for your blessed presence that surrounds me with love and fills me with peace.

If I Should Die Before I Wake

I love looking at the pictures. A DVD, actually, set to music and quite professional with dissolves and close-ups and fade-outs. The night they were taken was the worst of my life. But when I watch the soft images on my screen, all I remember are the blessings—the beauty and sanctity. These glimpses document the eternal connection we have with Jackson.

My pregnancy was normal, just like the other two. So nothing prepared me for the complications at delivery.

I lay there, helpless, as they worked on him, trying to get him to breathe. They hooked him to a respirator just before whisking him to the neonatal ICU. Terror squeezed my heart when the hospital chaplain came to pray with Nate and me.

The next few hours were a blur. CT scan, blood work, neurologists. When they finally allowed it, Nate wheeled me to the NICU. Even through the tubes and wires that crisscrossed his tiny body, we could see that Jackson was beautiful, perfect—except for the breathing.

And not moving. He couldn't open his eyes. He made no new-baby fist to grasp our fingers. If he couldn't hold on to us, we would hold on to him. I caressed his fuzzy head and kissed his fingers and toes. Nate whispered reassurances into the baby's seashell ears. We smiled at this wondrous creation. We prayed in faith. We cried in fear.

Then the seizures started.

New tests were ordered. When the results came back, our entire world fell apart.

"There's no hope." The doctor shook his head, but not before we noticed the moisture in his eyes. Jackson had touched his heart, too. "Take as much time as you need."

Time? I needed a future, the dream fulfilled of adding this baby to our family, discovering his personality, uncovering his talents. I needed . . . I needed . . .

"Pictures," said Nate.

"What?"

"There's a gallery of newborns in the hallway." He squeezed my hand. "We need pictures. I'll call the photographer listed."

When Joyce arrived, we explained our needs. "What I really want are pictures without the respirator." Her brow knit in consternation. "I don't want to remember him this way."

In spite of her uncertainties, this sensitive photographer agreed to our plan and set up in the little room next door. With leaden hearts, we asked the nurse to disconnect Jackson's tubes.

There was a holy stillness at the photo shoot. Joyce's ministrations were whisper soft as she positioned Jackson and me chest to chest. She urged me to rock, cuddle, and croon. She tilted our heads and curved our hands. She slipped our wedding bands on his delicate hand.

Every suggestion was thoughtfully planned and tenderly completed, in spite of the tears coursing down her cheeks. Joyce hugged us when she was done and slipped from the room.

Empty and broken, Nate and I held Jackson a bit longer, whispering our good-byes, stroking his lips, choking on our

grief, so reluctant to let him go. He never even took a breath. Never moved. Never opened his eyes.

But now, now, I have the compassionate slide show Joyce produced. I take time to admire the dimple in Jackson's chin, the swirl of red hair at his crown, the heart-shape birthmark at the nape of his neck.

Thanks to Joyce's ministry and her angel-like care of our son, Jackson is forever a part of our family, no matter how brief his stay.

ANGELS ARE EVERYWHERE, WAITING TO HELP US THROUGH THE HARDEST OF TIMES. ALL WE NEED TO DO IS ASK FOR THEIR HELP AND BELIEVE WE WILL RECEIVE IT.

Heavenly Father,

We thank you for your holy angels, both those in heaven and those with human names and faces. They make our lives more bearable in times of trouble, and they add to our joy in the good times.

Keep us always in your sight, Lord. When we stumble, please send your merciful messengers to pick us up again. When we are lost, send them to light the way home.

Amen

Lucille

Esther was struggling to care for her husband, Al. He had suffered a severe stroke, and he could no longer be left alone. Esther was feeling overwhelmed and exhausted. Al wanted more than anything to stay in his own home, and Esther was trying to fulfill his wishes. She was just barely making it through every day.

Lucille and John had been acquaintances of Al and Esther. They had various small-town connections but had never been close friends. A friend of a friend had explained to Lucille what Esther was going through and that she needed help. That was all Lucille needed to hear. She called Esther that very afternoon and asked what she could do to make things easier.

From that moment on, Esther heard from Lucille every day. Lucille did everything from grocery shopping to walking the dog to sitting with Al so that Esther could nap or pay bills or get outside. Some days, Lucille cleaned the house.

Esther didn't know what to say, other than thank you. It was like the Lord had sent Lucille. Some days, Esther had to tell her *not* to come over because she was afraid she'd get burned out and not come back. Lucille understood and would back off a little. But whenever anything important was needed, she was there.

There was one thing in particular that seemed an extra burden to Esther—but Al took such pleasure in it, she never would've complained. Al loved looking at the miniature cars that he picked out and ordered online. He could sit with one of his little cars on his lap for hours. There wasn't really a good

place to keep the cars, though, and Esther ended up packing them into a little box every night and unpacking them again in the morning.

One afternoon, Lucille and John showed up at the door with a custom-made, lighted bookshelf—specially designed to hold the car collection in a way that Al could see them from his easy chair in the family room. Al was delighted with the shelf, and Esther was especially happy to have one less chore to do every night.

It just seemed like whatever they needed, Lucille was always right there—whether it was sweeping the floor, an encouraging word and prayer, or a new pair of socks. She just kept helping right up until Al finally couldn't fight anymore. He developed pneumonia and was gone before they really knew what had happened.

Lucille and John were around, of course, right after Al died. They helped with cleaning the house and making phone calls and arrangements. And then they helped with cleaning the house after the funeral, when all the relatives had gone home.

And then nothing. Esther didn't hear from Lucille. She left messages for her and never got a reply. At first she was a bit concerned, then she felt rather hurt. Finally she realized that Lucille had been there for her when she needed help the most. Now she needed other things, but they were not the kind of help that Lucille offered.

When Esther last heard, Lucille had found a new family to help. It seems that sometimes, angels walk around the earth disguised as regular people.

**GOD'S ANGELS ARE MESSENGERS,
GIVING US COMFORT AND ASSURANCE OF
GOD'S PRESENCE IN ANY SHADOWY VALLEY
THROUGH WHICH WE MAY WALK.**

Father,

It's not always clear to me why suffering comes. But it is clear to me that whenever I do suffer, you are close at hand. I can see you in the kindnesses you deliver to me through your angels. Some angels are strangers, some are friends, some are unseen, but all remind me that you see me, that you care for me, that you are with me.

Amen

**WHEN YOU ARE ANGRY WITH SOMEONE,
REMEMBER, BOTH OF YOUR GUARDIAN ANGELS
ARE HOLDING THE SAME OLIVE BRANCH OF PEACE.**

Matchmaker

Divorce had never been something Mary imagined she'd go through, but here she was, holding her final dissolution papers two years to the day after her husband left her for another woman. Mary felt sad and alone even though her marriage had not been a good one; her husband had been unfaithful many times.

But now she had to wonder whether she would ever find love again. She was a middle-aged woman with two children and a full-time job. How on earth would she ever be able to find the time or the courage to love someone again? She knew that it would be a long time before her closed heart would open, especially with two children to think about.

The nights were loneliest for Mary, and she would lie awake wondering what it would be like to share her life with someone. Often, she would cry herself to sleep, resigned to the fact that she just might end up one of those bitter women who never remarry and go around condemning men for the rest of her life.

Her office complex was bustling with energy. One day— months after her divorce—as people rushed to and from their offices, Mary caught sight of a nice-looking man, about her age, sitting on a bench near the courtyard fountain. He was reading the newspaper and looked as though, amid all the craziness, he had not a care in the world. He looked up at Mary and their eyes met, just for a moment. Mary blushed and turned away, rushing into her office to face another pile of work. It never seemed to get any smaller, that pile.

That night, Mary prayed as usual for her children and her family. And she even prayed for herself, that she might find happiness again. As she did, she felt a soft sensation envelop her, and she felt loved and comforted. She opened her eyes, but there was nothing there.

A week later, Mary saw him again. He was dressed in casual attire, obviously employed by one of the companies in her complex. He was sitting at the fountain, reading, only this time, when he caught Mary's eye, he smiled and waved. Mary waved back, feeling self-conscious, but she found herself being pushed by some unseen force in his direction.

They introduced themselves, and soon Mary found herself accepting an invitation to coffee with this man named Hal. He was a lawyer in a firm in the same building as Mary's own company, where she worked as a marketing manager. They shared coffee later that evening, then dinner, and conversation that lasted for hours. Mary felt suddenly young again and full of hope and promise. But she also felt herself pulling back and feeling that usual lack of self-worth, that cautiousness that came from being hurt so deeply once before.

She prayed again that night for a sign about whether she should continue to see Hal. But she fell asleep without any great insights. The next morning, Mary got the kids off to school, realizing in the light of day that she was better off alone so she could focus on her children. They needed her and she had to give them what little time she had left after work each day. Still, her heart longed to connect . . . to someone.

Mary continued to work, take care of her kids, and visit friends when time permitted. The loneliness became more of

a numb ache, and she tried her best to just ignore it and focus instead on her day-to-day business. But it was always in front of her, other couples out having fun, showing each other signs of affection, loving each other. Mary became certain that she had had her one shot at love, and it had not been a success. Still, she went to bed each night and prayed for a sign.

So much for signs, she thought, until she spotted Hal sitting at his usual spot, waiting for her. And behind him, she saw a glimmer of light. Was it a ray of sunshine? Or could it be an angel beckoning her?

Mary was convinced in that moment she and Hal would be together for the rest of their lives. She sat down beside him, and he smiled and took her hand in his. Mary glanced quickly above Hal, but she no longer saw the light shining. Still, she had gotten her sign. This time, she truly believed that love had found her. After all, she had the approval of her angel, and whom could she trust more to pick out her soul mate?

Mary and Hal were married six months later in a beautiful ceremony by a lovely fountain in the courtyard of a church. Close friends and family attended, and Mary's two children beamed with pride and happiness for their mom. Mary was forever grateful for her matchmaker angel.

ENCOURAGEMENT IS ONE OF THE MOST POWERFUL THINGS ANGELS BRING TO OUR LIVES.

Our Father's Legacy Is for the Birds

On the first anniversary of our father's death, my sister and I returned to his grave for the first time. It was a seven-hour drive, and propping a wreath by his headstone seemed too meager an homage to the man who had tolerated our teenage insanities and discretely loaned us money when we were broke.

My sister suggested that we visit his favorite charity, a place he had taken us to and the organization he had specified where all memorial gifts should be sent. In his retirement, our father, who had always loved birds, had found a struggling little nonprofit organization that rescued injured birds of prey: eagles, falcons, and owls. He even liked the buzzards, ugly and grotesque, and he had warned us that they often vomit on visitors and can hit their targets up to 20 feet away.

Eileen, the director of the shoestring operation, remembered us and talked fondly of our father. "Earl was our grandfather," she said. "He not only gave us money, he raised money from local businesses. He kept our old van running, repaired cages, and gave presentations to schools to educate children about raptors." We knew he donated money to the cause, and we knew he liked to release birds when they were ready to return to the wild. We did not know about his other activities.

Eileen took us to see our dad's favorite raptor, Churchill, a magnificent bald eagle. He could not be released because he was imprinted on humans and would not be able to survive on his own. Our dad's name was engraved on a plaque on Churchill's cage. "That's the first raptor your dad adopted," Eileen said. "He gave us the flight cage, too. But, girls, there is something else you should know."

We tore our eyes away from the stately eagle. "I'm not a churchgoer," Eileen said, "and I never had any reason to believe in answered prayers." She paused as if waiting for permission to continue. Churchill screeched. We nodded encouragement. "Well, shortly after your dad died, our van conked out again, fortunately in the driveway. My son said it was the fan belt. That night I tried to figure out how to pay for repairs, but it was the end of the month and we were already in the red. The next morning, my son noticed the hood was partway open. He thought he had closed it, but he took another look inside. A new fan belt had been installed, and the van ran just fine."

"Dad was a good mechanic," I said, surprised that I was not all that surprised.

"Then when the buzzards clawed a hole in the flight cage, I didn't have to call a carpenter because the next morning new boards had been nailed over the hole."

"He was good with home repairs," my sister said.

Eileen took a deep breath. "Just last week, the vet bill arrived. I was expecting my worst nightmare thanks to a buzzard with a broken wing and three sick owls, but I also remembered that he had made an emergency call when we thought Churchill was dying."

I looked at the eagle. "Looks like he survived. Dad would be happy about that."

"You think he doesn't know?" Eileen said. "That morning, when all I could see was a rising tide of red ink, I stamped my foot and yelled, "Earl! You know I can't pay this bill. Do something!"

"What did he do?" my sister asked.

"I have no idea," Eileen said. "All I know is less than an hour later I got a call from a local business owner. He said your dad had visited him two years ago and asked him to support us. The man was not interested then and stuck our business card in a desk drawer. He said when he got to work that morning, the card was on his desk, faceup, and he had been wondering on the way to the office what to do about a tax write-off he needed to make."

"Wow!" I said, "How much did he ante up?"

"He not only paid the outstanding vet bill, he said he would cover our vet bills for at least a year—all of them." She sounded both awed and perplexed.

"Sounds like you still have a grandfather," I said.

Eileen nodded. "Amazing, isn't it? It's like he never really left us."

My sister turned to look at Churchill again. "And we brought a wreath," she muttered. "A stupid wreath for an empty grave." The eagle made a guttural noise that sounded like disgust.

That was the last wreath we laid on our father's grave. Instead of remembering our father with flowers, we each adopted a buzzard: She chose Attila and I chose The Hun. Eileen said she wanted to have our names engraved on plaques for their cages. She handed us a piece of paper and told us

to write our names so she would have them spelled correctly. My sister and I had a brief, private conversation. The paper we returned to Eileen said only, "Earl's daughters."

We tell friends we adopted two ugly buzzards and encourage them to adopt one of the beautiful birds of prey. We show them photos of spotted owls and peregrine falcons. We don't need to raise funds for Churchill. He already has a grandfather.

SOMETIMES A LOVING ANGEL IS BORN OF OUR SADNESS, AND WE ARE HEALED.

To My Guardian Angel—

I'm sorry if I get frustrated or upset with you these days.
I know I must not always be the easiest person to be a
Guardian Angel for.
It's just that I'm having a hard time right now.
And sometimes I forget how truly blessed I am—
and how good you are to me.
Please be patient with me.
Help see me through to better times.

*T*rapped!

The entire town under a tornado warning, and Jessica did what she could to batten down the hatches as high winds from the massive hurricane ripped through the Gulf. Already, three neighboring towns had suffered severe damage from both the hurricane itself and the many twisters it spawned once it made landfall. It was only a matter of time before Jessica had to either get out or buckle down, and she figured at this point, it was too late to evacuate.

Living in the Gulf region had made Jessica wary of harsh weather, and she had already survived some of the biggest storms nature had to offer. This one felt different, though. Her town had always managed to slip between the cracks when tornadoes moved through, but she could feel the strange sensation of doom approaching as the skies outside her small suburban home darkened to a muddy brown-green.

She never heard the warning sirens. Jessica felt the beast coming as her ears popped from the pressure changes. Then she heard it, that awful sound that could only be described as an oncoming locomotive. She fled into the safety of her laundry room. She had no basement, but often used the laundry room for shelter since it was the innermost room with the strongest supporting walls.

Outside, the sounds became deafening as the tornado swirled closer. Jessica could hear walls and roofs being torn from their foundations and tossed like bottle caps across the street and beyond. She cringed, angry at herself for not getting out sooner and heading to the town's emergency shelter. She

had been through this so many times before, and nothing had ever happened.

This time, she wasn't so lucky, as the full force of the F4 bore down on her home, raising the entire frame off its foundation and blasting wood and glass to smithereens. Jessica prayed loudly as she held on to the doorframe, but the winds took hold of her like a child's balloon, and she felt the bizarre sensation of floating through the sky.

Then everything went black.

When Jessica came to, she had no idea where she was, except that she was in total darkness and she could not move. Her body was covered in debris, and she ached when she tried to lift an arm or raise a leg. She peered through two large beams of wood and saw the black night sky above, now almost clear. Stars peeked out at her, and she realized the storm had passed. How long had she been out?

She could hear the voices of people screaming out names, shouting for help. She thought she saw the red flash of emergency lights, but when she tried to cry out for help, her voice was raspy. No one could hear her unless they were right on top of her, and the voices were getting further away, not closer.

Closing her eyes, Jessica prayed that someone would find her before morning. She didn't know if she would survive the long night and wondered if the eye of the hurricane was the reason for the clear skies. If it began to rain again, she might drown in this hole before someone could get to her.

She had no idea how severely she was injured, although it worried her that she could not feel one leg at all. She began to weep as she realized she could no longer hear the voices. They were moving too far away from her.

The stars above twinkled, and Jessica felt a sudden breeze trickle between the beams of wood that trapped her. A glow of light filled the hole she was in, and her heart leapt, thinking help had finally arrived. A man leaned over the beams and peered down at her.

"I'm here to get you out," he said, and his voice calmed Jessica immediately.

The man began to lift debris off Jessica, single-handedly, and Jessica had to wonder how he could be strong enough to move some of the slabs of wood and heavy furniture that blocked her from freedom. But he did, and within minutes he was carrying Jessica over to the road. He set her gently down and used his cell phone to call 911. Within minutes, an ambulance was on the scene and Jessica was loaded in and taken to the county hospital.

As the paramedics loaded her, she weakly asked one of them if she could get the man's name who rescued her. She wanted to make sure she thanked him properly later.

But the paramedic just looked at her strangely.

"Miss, you were on the side of the road all alone when we found you," he said.

"But he called 911. Didn't you get the call?" Jessica asked, feeling dizzy and weak.

"No, Miss. We were checking the neighborhood and saw you lying here."

They closed the doors to the ambulance and sped off, leaving Jessica to wonder about the man who set her free. She closed her eyes and thanked God for sending her an angel to find her, and she prayed that others trapped in debris were finding their own angels coming to their rescue.

A Needed Break

A retired librarian and researcher, Joan Allen had a number of things she wanted to do while she was still able. One of them was to learn how to paint with watercolors. She had recently begun to make scrapbooks with her photographs, but she wanted a bit more of a challenge, and painting seemed to provide that.

But as a caregiver to her 100-year-old mother, she was on duty 24 hours a day. "I have to perform a medical procedure on Mom four times a day at specific intervals, including one at 4:00 A.M.," she said. "Some days those six-hour intervals telescope into what seems like only an hour."

In addition, her mom is hard of hearing and her memory is failing. Joan said, "She has to be reminded four or five times to take her pills or to drink her water or to eat her meals. I've become such a nag I can't stand myself."

Some nights her mother wakes her from a sound sleep three or four times, so Joan also often feels sleep-deprived.

"My husband helps me as much as he can," Joan said, "but he has a chronic illness that flares up regularly and keeps him anemic and very weak. A medicine he takes for flare-ups causes a serious side-effect, so he must go on additional medication." One time last year both her husband and her Mom were in the hospital in the same week.

"My duties aren't difficult, just boring and repetitive and sometimes frustrating. The highlight of my day is running to the grocery store. I long for the chance to do something creative."

She wanted to pursue her interest in watercolor painting but found it difficult to find opportunities for classes that fit in with her Mom's schedule.

Joan took a few classes locally during her mother's nap time, but what she really wanted to do was take a class in botanical art, given at the arboretum some distance away.

"Dream on," Joan told herself. No matter what time those classes were held, with the commute time factored in, she couldn't work them around her mom's medical procedure.

She tried to practice painting on her own, but she needed instruction to help her improve. One of her former teachers encouraged her to enroll in a certificate program. "It would take a miracle to make that happen," Joan responded.

Last spring Joan confided in one of her instructors at the nearby art school about her dream of taking the botanical art course. A few months later, she opened the school's newsletter and found that the course she wanted was being given locally, condensed as a four-day workshop. What's more, it was being taught by the same person who taught the course at the arboretum—and it fit into her mom's schedule. She enrolled immediately.

"It sounds to me like a real, live angel was at work here," Joan joked. "Two, if you count my husband, who gave Mom her lunch and tucked her in for her nap each day."

Joan attended the workshop all four days and found it to be both soul-satisfying and valuable. "It was a gift. I loved it!" she said. "The only problem is that now I have a bigger passion for art than ever and would like to continue. I don't want to be selfish, but maybe my angel wouldn't mind helping me again so I can take another class before I get too old?"

Night and Day

A full, dark year of things going wrong. Beverly's brow creased in concern. *Getting fired was humiliating, but nothing compared to backed up rent, losing the apartment, sleeping in the car.*

With the nights getting colder, they needed a roof over their heads. She needed a job, a way to keep everyone fed. The problems seemed bigger than her. She felt hopeless.

Then she overheard a conversation at the soup kitchen, and that brought her to this place. She read the sign: Angel House.

"Stick close and stay quiet," she urged the kids and opened the door. A robust woman greeted them. "Tell me your story." She handed Beverly a steaming mug of coffee and directed the kids to the playroom.

Relieved, Beverly poured out her problems.

"Well, we're only a day center," the director explained, "but we've contracted with local churches to provide hot meals and shelter at night."

"Food? Beds?" Beverly's eyes rounded at the prospect.

"Yes. Even hot showers. But it's only a temporary fix. And you must commit to budgeting classes and career counseling."

Even as she agreed to the outlined conditions, Beverly's heart thumped at the possibilities. Once she got back on her feet, she knew she could find another job and provide for her family again. The woman handed her a sheaf of forms. "Remember, it's only temporary."

But Beverly knew she was being offered more than a place to lay their heads. Angel House gave her something she thought she'd lost: Hope.

The Night of Two Angels

Katy Barnes was 12 years old and a seventh-grader at Nobel School in Chicago when she was diagnosed with pleural pneumonia. In those years before sulfa and penicillin, it was a very serious illness requiring hospitalization. She was wheeled into a room for a fluoroscope and later remembered two technicians talking about one of the X-rays.

"Looks bad, doesn't it?" said one.

"Yeah. I'd say she has about a 50–50 chance," the other answered.

Surely they can't be talking about me? Katy thought. Someone told her about another girl across the hall who had the same ailment, so Katy presumed they were talking about her. All she knew was that she was very tired and had an aching back.

"You have fluid around your lungs and it must be removed," said her doctor, wielding a huge syringe. "But don't worry. I'll give you something to numb your back. You won't feel a thing." He plunged in the needle.

"Now I know what it feels like to be stabbed in the back, but without the pain," Katy told her parents later.

Katy remembered how hungry she felt that evening. She consumed a large tray of food and relished every bite, while the other patient across the hall could not or would not eat anything.

When her mom came back the next morning, Katy felt a whole lot better, but when she tried to tell her mother how she felt, the words came out all wrong. She knew what she wanted

to say, but when she spoke she didn't make sense. Her mother cried. In hushed tones, the nurse talked about "delirium" and "crisis." Her mom left with a worried look.

The next thing Katy knew, Clara, her mom's friend from church, came to stay with her that night. Katy thought Clara, a nurse, looked like a plump angel, with her hair in a bun and her glasses sliding down her nose and resting on her round cheeks.

Clara put cool wet cloths on her head and offered her glasses of sweet orange juice. It felt good to see Clara's smiling face every time she opened her eyes.

That night Katy became very tired. She remembered closing her eyes and walking down a long, dark tunnel.

Am I going to die? she wondered. It was eerie and lonely there in the tunnel, but she thought she saw another girl walking ahead of her into the light.

Then Katy heard a voice speaking to her. "You can go back now," it said. "It's not your time."

She remembered turning and walking back down the tunnel. Then she thought: *Was that an angel talking to me? Where is the other girl?*

When she woke up, the first thing Katy saw was Clara's cherubic face. Clara smiled and said, "Welcome back. Would you like something to eat?" When Katy nodded, Clara brought her a tray of eggs, toast, and juice. It tasted so good, Katy wanted to ask for more, but she didn't.

Clara hugged her, gathered up her own belongings and said, "I must go now. I'll see you in a couple of weeks at church."

Katy waved good-bye. When her mom came to see Katy that afternoon, she was all smiles.

"Did something good happen?" Katy asked her.

"Yes," said Mom. "The crisis is past. You're going to get better." Then she hugged Katy.

"Momma," Katy confessed. "I saw an angel last night."

Mom nodded. "Oh, you mean Miss Clara?"

"Her, too," said Katy. "But there was this other angel who told me to go back because it wasn't time."

Katy noticed her mother wiping her eyes.

"How is the other girl, across the hall?" she asked.

Her mom just shook her head and didn't answer.

Katy is now 75 years old, but she still remembers the night when two angels came to visit her. One gave her comfort and the other helped her live.

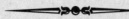

THE ANGEL OF FAITH HELPS US TRUST GOD
DESPITE OUR CIRCUMSTANCE.

THE ANGEL OF HOPE HELPS US PRESS ON
THROUGH OUR CIRCUMSTANCE.

BUT THE ANGEL OF GOD'S LOVE HOLDS US
IN OUR CIRCUMSTANCE.

Pieced Together

She picked idly at the loose button on her favorite blouse and stared at it without blinking. She should get out a needle and thread and tighten it, she supposed, but it simply took too much effort.

Nights were the worst. The kids exhausted her during the day, but once they were bedded down the empty evening stretched endlessly before her. Not that there wasn't stuff to do—take this button, for instance. In fact, with a growing family there was more to do than two people could accomplish.

But that was the problem. There weren't two. There was only one.

At first she'd tried to pretend he was still deployed. That actually worked for a while. After all, she and the little ones were used to his tours of duty and everything it entailed: writing e-mails, sending care packages, taking turns during the occasional phone calls. The children especially liked posing for those silly photographs she posted on the computer to entertain Joe and remind him that they were waiting for him to come home.

Last time, all four kids contorted themselves into alphabet shapes and had her snap pictures until, side by side, the laughing little human letters spelled out WE LOVE YOU. Then, with the quick press of the Send button, she had e-mailed it to the faraway place that was always so near in her mind: Iraq.

The memory wrenched a sob from her. *Did Joe see it? Did he have time to check his e-mail that morning before... before...*

They said the blast that killed Joe came from another crazy suicide bomber. But, somehow, she couldn't wrap her mind around the idea that someone thought so little of his own life that he was willing to sacrifice it for the sole purpose of taking the lives of others.

Her other. Her other half. Her Joe.

She gave a fierce tug at the loose button and watched it fall into her hand. *It didn't make sense.*

But then, nothing made sense lately. Even this place. Fort Drum wasn't much different than any other army base, and she was used to finding friends wherever the whim of the military sent them. Only this time she hadn't even settled in when Joe was deployed. They'd spent every precious last minute together as a family, right up to the moment they waved good-bye when he boarded the plane. And then the bombing occurred only a few days after he arrived in the Middle East.

Everything happened quickly. Not that it stopped women from showing up when they heard the news. Military wives care for their own, finding strength in sisterhood. They arrived promptly at her doorstep. With casseroles. With offers to help. A couple of them even volunteered to dispose of Joe's clothes.

The clothes he'll never need again. The thought was like a bullet piercing the emotional dam she'd erected and her ready tears gushed through the hole.

She pressed a pillow to her mouth to muffle the wailing she could no longer contain. She kept it there so the noise wouldn't startle and wake the children.

Joe, Joe, I miss you so much. I want you back. I want you home. The kids need you. I need you. She felt hollow and so alone. *I want your arms around me, holding me.*

When her sobs waned to an occasional hiccup, she drifted into an exhausted sleep on the overstuffed couch. But a soft, persistent rapping at the front door roused her.

Someone's here? She glanced at her wristwatch. *At nine o'clock?*

She smoothed her hair and unlocked the door. "Yes?" She recognized the faces but didn't know their names.

"We're sorry to come by so late." The two women on the stoop eyed her puffy face. "But we have something for you and felt an urgency to deliver it tonight."

"For me? Come in."

The women placed a soft mound on the dining room table. "Suzy and Krista brought us your husband's clothes and . . ."

Suzy? Krista? Then she connected the names to the ones who'd packed up and disposed of Joe's personal things.

". . . we're members of Going to Pieces, the quilting guild here at Fort Drum." They smiled. "We—all of us—made this for you."

One of the ladies spread open the bundle on the table and smoothed its folds.

"From Joe's clothes?" Her eyes widened in wonder at the quilt. "You made this from his clothes?" She traced a block with a trembling finger. Pieces of desert-sand camouflage, fatigues, dress uniforms.

The women nodded. "Every piece came from your husband's slacks and shirts. The pattern we chose is Lover's Knot.

It seemed—symbolic." They lifted the quilt and wrapped it around her shoulders.

She snuggled an edge to her cheek and closed her eyes. "It's like Joe's arms," she whispered. "Like he's here, holding me again."

When she finally looked up, the women were gone.

I didn't thank them, and I don't even know their names. She frowned in consternation.

Then her brow cleared. It didn't matter. She knew who they were. She had recognized them by the goodness shining from their eyes and the empathy spilling from their hearts.

Lord,

In times of weakness and doubt, help us remember that you are always capable of miracles. Keep us ever alert to the possibility of visits from your ministering angels whom you send to protect and guide us.

May we receive them with a joyous and grateful heart and then pass on the blessings to others who need their comfort.

Amen

ANGELS DON'T ALWAYS HAVE WINGS;
SOMETIMES THEY HAND US HANKIES
AND GIVE US SHOULDERS TO CRY ON.

These hard times help me see with new eyes, Lord. Despite my tears, I see more clearly your tender mercies, my great need for your presence, and the angels in my life I had overlooked or would never have otherwise seen. Thank you for opening my eyes, even as you comfort my heart.

YOU'LL MEET MORE ANGELS AS YOU TRUDGE A RUGGED PATH
THROUGH A FOGGY FOREST THAN YOU WILL WALKING DOWN A
SIDEWALK ON A WARM, SUNNY DAY.

The Lady in the Yellow Dress

Sitting beside my father's hospital bed, I reflected that there were three graces in his dying. One, he had lived to age 86; two, he had had little pain and seemed to be going peacefully; and three, after 30 years, he would be reunited with my mother. He had loved her so much and missed her so keenly that the thought of their reunion soothed a great deal of my pain. If it was true, that is. If they really would be reunited. If what I understood of God was correct. I thought I knew, but how could anyone ever be sure? That it would just end, that his last breath would simply erase their great love was a thought that made me cringe. Yet the thought nibbled at me, taking sharper bites as his breathing slowed. A nurse came in, checked him and said, "It won't be long now."

I knew I needed to be with him when he died, more for me than for him; he had been unresponsive for three days. I had been up all night, and it was close to lunchtime. My daughter had arrived early that morning with Jamie, my five-year-old grandson. We agreed that the experience was not scary for the child, particularly when Jamie said, "Hi, Papa, I brought my coloring book." He seemed to understand that his Papa was too sick to talk. He settled down while I sat beside my father in a hard, straight-back chair so I would not fall asleep.

My daughter gave up trying to get me to take a break and went to the cafeteria for a carryout lunch we could eat in the hospital room. Jamie requested a hamburger, but all I wanted was coffee. I was beyond exhausted, but I could not release my father's hand, not when he was so close to the end. Maybe he would revive a little, say a last word. Maybe there would be time for a last kiss. I clutched his hand harder and willed myself to remain alert.

And then I jerked awake. My hand had slipped away from his, and I saw he was no longer breathing. I could not speak or move. I could not feel anything but numb, as if I had stumbled and had all the wind knocked out of me.

"Grandma?" Jamie said. Slowly, I turned to him. He was holding a yellow crayon. "Papa left," he said calmly as if his grandfather had just run out to the store for a quart of milk.

"Left?" I was too dazed to make any sense out of it, too weary to try to understand.

"He left with the lady," Jamie said. "When they got to the door, they waved good-bye."

I turned back to my father and felt feeling return to my hands as they patted his shoulder, to my heart as it began to break, to my eyes as they filled with tears. "What lady?" I asked, my voice barely a whisper.

Jamie looked up from his coloring book. "I don't know, but she was real pretty and she had on a yellow dress." He held up his crayon. "Like this. I'm coloring her dress now."

I looked at his book, but the yellow was just a kindergartner's scrawl.

My daughter walked into the room with a lunch tray. I took it from her before I told her that her grandfather had passed away. I held her while she sobbed, feeling much stronger now. "Your grandmother came for him," I said. "Jamie saw them walk out the door."

"Jamie?" she said, "What, exactly, did you see?"

"Did you get me a hamburger?" he asked, as if nothing remarkable had occurred.

My daughter settled him in the family waiting room and then returned to kiss her grandfather and help me wash his hands and face. "I know it's a cliché," she said, "but he really does look peaceful."

"Pam, do you believe Jamie?"

"I don't know why he would make something like that up."

"He's never seen the photo album of my mother in her yellow dress," I said. "It's been somewhere in the attic since before he was born."

"I seem to remember that photo," she said. "They were leaving for a cruise and she was wearing a yellow dress."

"Their last cruise," I said. "We buried her in that dress."

The nurses came in and asked us to leave the room. I kissed my father's forehead and squeezed his hand. Pam and I sat with Jamie while he finished his hamburger.

"He certainly doesn't look traumatized," Pam said. "Jamie, are you feeling okay, now that your Papa has gone?"

"When is he coming back?" Jamie asked.

My daughter looked stricken and turned to me for help.

"Oh, he'll be back all right, and he'll be with the pretty lady in the yellow dress," I said. "But they won't be back for a long time, 20 or 25 years maybe." After all, I was only 60, and I expected to live for another two decades or more.

The Skid

I squinted between swipes of the icy wipers and fought to keep my station wagon between the craggy rock wall on my left and the sheer drop to my right. Just like my life, I thought.

I'd spent the day in the high country, confiding the horrific details of my secret life to a caring friend: my husband's escalating anger, my fear and humiliation . . . and eventual escape. I felt so alone, frightened of any new relationship.

"I'm so proud you left him," she said as she hugged me good-bye. "But, remember, not every man is an abuser. You've got to trust again."

With the roads freezing over, I considered turning back. But a large boulder bounced from the side of the mountain just ahead of me. Chunks of broken rock ricocheted, and I slammed on my brakes to avoid them. The car skidded. I jerked the steering wheel.

Too far! But when I overcorrected, the car fishtailed down hairpin curves.

With clammy hands, I gripped the wheel and forced myself to stay calm, skid after skid. After a final slow-motion rotation, the car came to a crooked, shuddering stop.

Except for the gritty grind of wipers against ice, it was eerily quiet and I realized the noise that was missing was my own screams. I leaned my forehead against the steering wheel and swallowed the lump lodged in my throat.

In an effort to assess the situation, I tried to open the door but it was wedged against the base of the hill. From the pres-

sure on the left side of my body, I knew the car was lodged at an odd angle—with its nose buried in a juniper bush. I threw the gearshift into reverse. Nothing. I couldn't even rock the car loose.

That's when hysteria set in. There was no cell phone reception in this isolated canyon. And it was pointless to climb out of the car; where would I go?

"Oh, dear God, please send help. If ever I needed a guardian angel, it's now," I prayed out loud. I locked the doors and turned off the car to wait.

And wait.

When I got cold, I wondered what kind of miracle I was hoping for. It was after midnight now and everyone with any sense was home in bed. I shivered in my denim shirt and started the engine.

How long can I let the car idle without fear of asphyxiation? As soon as I was warm, I switched it off.

A long hour passed. And another. I burrowed into a ball and dozed.

Someone rapped on my window. "You okay in there?"

I jerked awake. The man loomed large under his Stetson. I couldn't see his face, but he was bulky and bearded.

Murderer? Druggie? Rapist? He could be any or all of those things.

"Don't worry, ma'am," he soothed. "I'm here to help. Now, let's get you out."

You prayed for help, I reminded myself. *Now trust. Trust.*

Apprehensive but relieved, I let him take charge, this good Samaritan of the night. Haloed by the headlights from his

pickup, he lifted me through the passenger door, carried me to the warmth of his truck, and tenderly tucked me into a coarse blanket that smelled like horse—and heaven.

"Which way home?" he twinkled. "Up the mountain or down? Kinda hard to tell from the direction your car was pointed!"

"Down, thank you," I murmured from my woolly nest and closed my sleepy, trustful eyes.

Lord,

Send me an angel to guide me and guard me, to lead and direct me, to comfort and hold me.

Send me an angel who knows what my heart needs most and who always has the highest and best solutions to my most challenging problems.

Send me an angel to walk with me through the dark and hold my hand as I tread the rocky road of life.

Send me an angel soon, Lord.

Amen

An Angel for All Seasons

It didn't matter if six days out of the seven in the week there was nothing but dust in my mailbox at college. I knew that there would be at least one day that I would find a card, a letter, a newspaper clipping, a little package, or something interesting, fun, and thoughtful from my aunt Katy to let me know she was thinking of me. Even though being away from home was a monumental season in my life, it was punctuated by a good deal of loneliness and homesickness. But in her simple but significant way, she was there for me.

For a few years after college, Aunt Katy had me over on New Year's Eve to eat cheese balls, drink sparkling cider, and put together puzzles. That was the season when I was working lots of hours, and my social life was all but nonexistent. During that time, Aunt Katy was there for me whenever a celebration of any sort came around and I found myself without company.

I don't think she's ever missed a birthday card my whole life long. She could make me laugh joyously even when I didn't feel like smiling. She identified personally with my haplessness. She never condemned me even when I was sure she was taken aback by some things I told her about myself.

Every time the landscape on my journey thinned to a desertlike place, when other people disappeared, Aunt Katy and her support never did.

She's fixed in my heart as my angel for all seasons.

My Uncle, My Angel

When their father left home, Vince and his four older siblings were distraught. In time the other kids seemed to adjust, but Vince, the youngest and most sensitive, missed having a father around to talk to, play with, and hug.

His uncle Bill seemed to understand. He gave Vince plenty of hugs. He often took him for ice cream.

"We had long talks about anything and everything," said Vince. "It felt good. Whenever I had a problem, it was Uncle Bill I went to for advice. He taught me how to play ball, how to bowl, and he even took me fishing in the pond behind the apartment buildings."

When Vince was old enough, his uncle taught him how to drive a car. "Then, when it was time to get my license, he took me out every day after work to practice. Uncle Bill had two jobs and a family of his own, but he still made time for me."

Vince remembers that when he got older and times got tough for him financially, his uncle would hand him "a few bucks to tide him over."

"He was always there for me," Vince said.

At his uncle's funeral, Vince gave a touching and tearful eulogy, acknowledging the man who had been both a surrogate father and his guardian angel for more than a decade.

Vince has vowed to "make a difference" in the lives of others, just as his Uncle Bill made a difference in his life. As a tribute, he and his cousin, Uncle Bill's son, have formed a company that modifies homes to help the handicapped live more comfortable lives.

**WHENEVER YOU SEEK TO FIND REST
IN THE SANCTUARY OF GOD'S MERCY,
YOU WILL ALWAYS FIND AN ANGEL AT HAND,
READY TO CARRY YOU THERE.**

Dear God,

I need a host of angels to pull me out of this swamp of sorrow and the unrelenting darkness of grief. Please send your angels to shine their light on the beauty of your creation so I can have a few moments of joy today. Tomorrow may be easier, but I really do need as many angels as you can spare today.

Amen

**JUST BECAUSE WE CANNOT SEE THEM DOESN'T MEAN ANGELS
DON'T EXIST. WE SEE PROOF OF THEIR PRESENCE IN EVERY ACT
OF LOVING KINDNESS WE GIVE AND RECEIVE.**

Angels Working Overtime

Karen was slated to give a workshop in a city in Florida, far from home, when her husband, John, learned he had prostate cancer and would require treatment. After they had consoled one another and prayed together, she grabbed her address book and headed for the phone.

"I'm canceling the workshop," Karen sobbed. "How can we leave town with this hanging over our heads? And why did it have to happen now, just when everything was going so well?"

"I guess it's just my turn," he said bravely.

As Karen picked up the phone, John grabbed her hand.

"Honey, let's wait and see what develops. Then we can make a decision."

Reluctantly, she agreed and hung up the phone. But she knew she couldn't hide her anguish and teach her class without breaking down. It would be impossible.

In the coming weeks, test results brought more bad news. There was evidence of other cancers lurking in John's body. Of particular concern was one attached to the right kidney. That meant a kidney specialist had to be contacted.

As the date for the workshop loomed closer, John took more tests. Several suspicious images were ruled out as cancer sources, so his oncologist and internist began to search for a renal surgeon.

"This might take awhile," John's doctors warned. "Why don't you take your trip to Florida while we contact a surgeon and decide on strategy?"

John agreed, but when he told Karen, she flatly refused. "How can I do this when our lives are falling apart?"

Cradling her face in his hands, John looked deeply into her eyes. "Where is your faith?" he asked.

Ashamed, Karen nodded. She stopped crying and began praying for guidance and reassurance. A few days later, by the time they'd packed and put their luggage into the car, Karen was still feeling down, but her husband's positive attitude encouraged her.

As the two-day drive began, they listened to the radio, choosing only music that was cheerful and upbeat. They avoided thinking about sad events and tried to remember all the funny things that had happened in their lives together. As they laughed, some of the fear drained out of Karen. Still, she couldn't completely get rid of that feeling of dread that nagged her.

"Lord," she prayed silently, "please give us a sign of your presence and an angel to remind us of your love."

At John's urging, she closed her eyes for a short nap. When she awoke, they were approaching a railroad bridge, and something caught her eye. On the side of the bridge, in freshly painted letters two feet high, read the words, "Trust in God."

"Did you see what I just saw?" Karen asked her husband.

"I sure did!" He smiled. "I think your angel got here just ahead of you!" Karen's spirit soared. Was God answering her prayers already?

At the end of the day, they checked into a motel. Encouraged by the sign, they went out to dinner, then took a long walk and talked about all the blessings God had sent them:

good friends, a happy family, a supportive church community, and plenty of opportunities for service to others. They temporarily forgot their problems.

Back at the motel, Karen picked up the newspaper and turned to the crossword puzzle. After filling in a few words, she went on to the next clue. She did a double take when the clue referenced a Bible verse. Grabbing the Gideon Bible in the motel room, she looked up Isaiah 41:10: "Do not fear, for I am with you."

She shared it with John. "This is the second time God has spoken to us!" she marveled.

The next night, Karen again picked up the Bible. It fell open to Psalm 30, and she read verse 11: "You have turned my mourning into dancing . . . and clothed me with joy." Amazed, Karen silently showed the verse to John. His eyes opened wide.

"Wow," he said. "Our angels are working overtime!"

By the time they reached the conference, Karen was buoyed up and ready to go on with her workshop and to share her story of God's assurance.

When they returned home, John prepared for surgery to remove his kidney.

"We really lucked out in getting a top-flight surgeon for you," said John's internist. "It was the strangest thing. I tried repeatedly to get in touch with a friend of mine who is the head of urology at the teaching hospital in the city. I finally got him at midnight. He was in his car, and I was in mine.

"He told me you didn't have to go to a different hospital. We had the best doctor available right in our own neighborhood—a kidney transplant surgeon!"

"That's great, but I don't think it was luck," said John to the puzzled doctor.

After the surgery was over, the surgeon asked, "What do you want first, the good news or the bad?"

The bad news was, yes, the kidney was cancerous. The good news was that the cancer hadn't spread but was self-contained. John had an 85 percent chance for a cure.

After he healed from surgery, John successfully underwent radiation for the prostate cancer and had no side effects. He was able to drive himself to the hospital for treatment the entire seven weeks.

Twelve years later, John and Karen are grateful to God and those angel helpers who reassured them at a trying period in their lives—and who continue to pull them through difficult times.

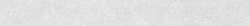

You know, Lord, lately I have been struggling just to get through the next hour, minute, second. Be merciful to me in my weakness and bring me strength and encouragement through the angels you send, faithful messengers of your compassion and comfort.

Amen